BOOK ONE

12 STEP Slogans & sayings

SOBRIETY COLORING BOOK

FOR ADULTS WORKING THE TWELVE STEPS

MW01170568

Questions, feature requests, suggestions: teetotalerpress@gmail.com

THIS COLORING BOOK BELONGS TO:

_____

One color, one day at a time!

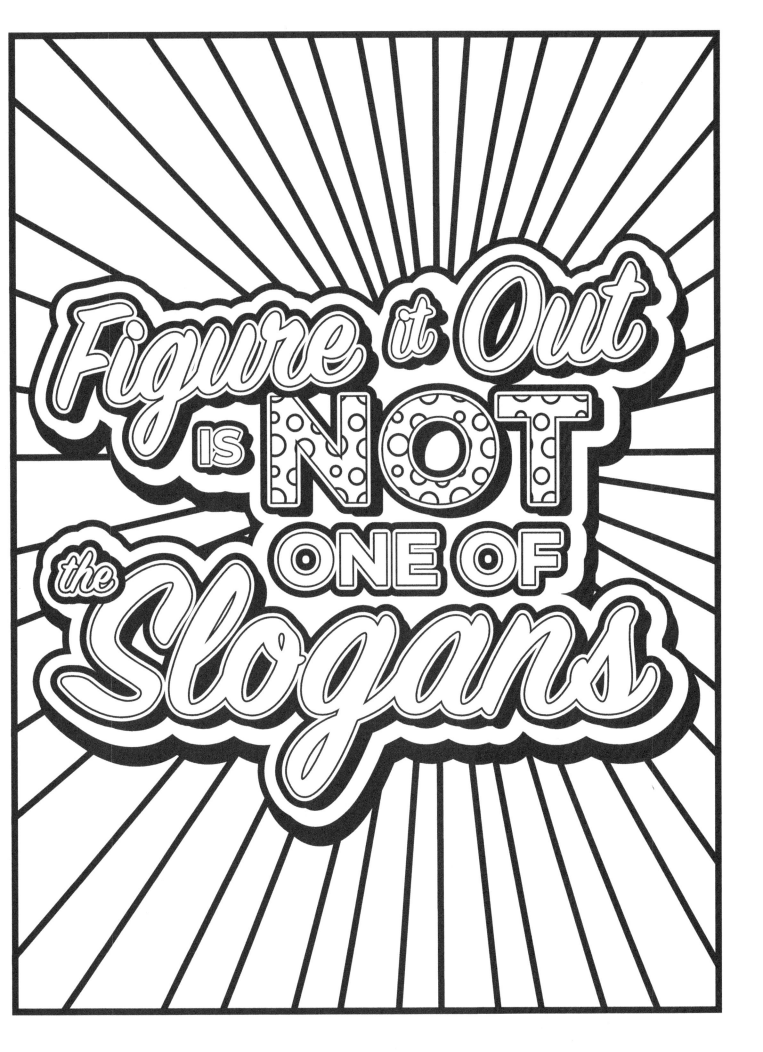

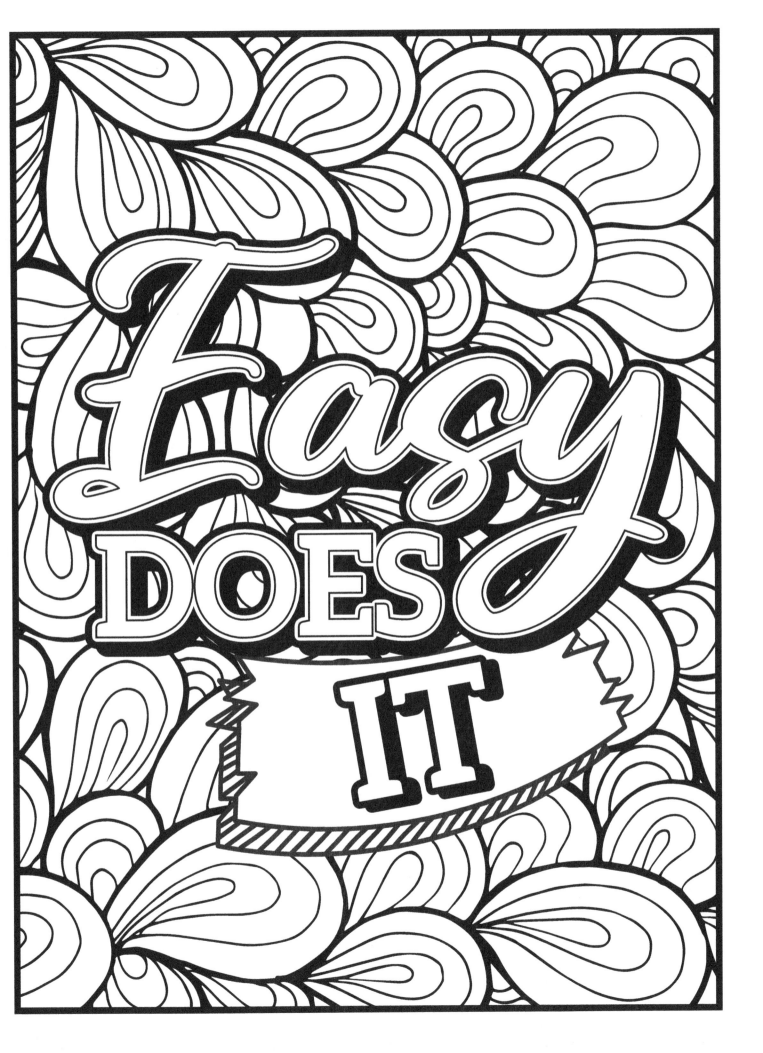

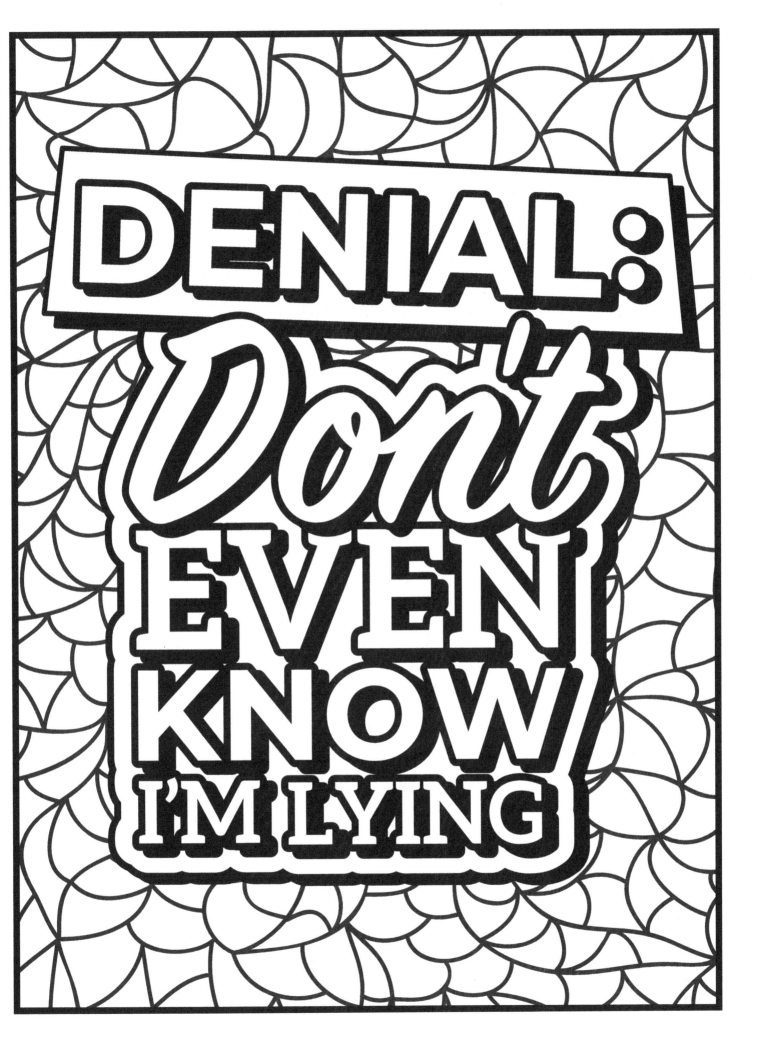

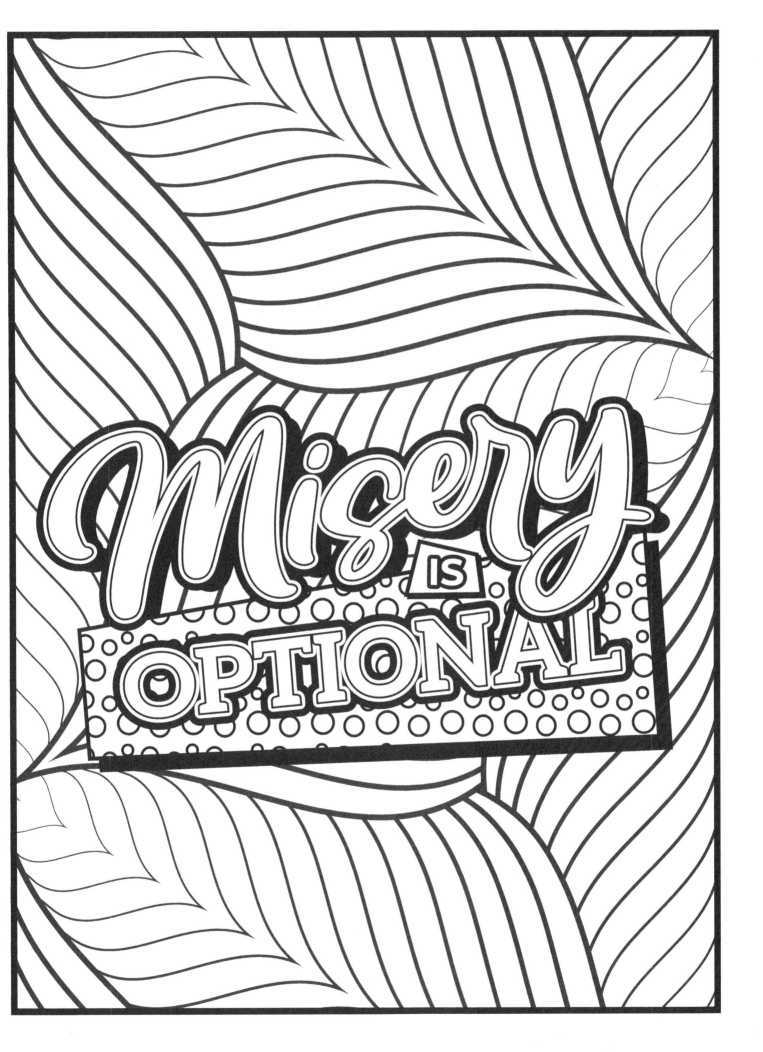

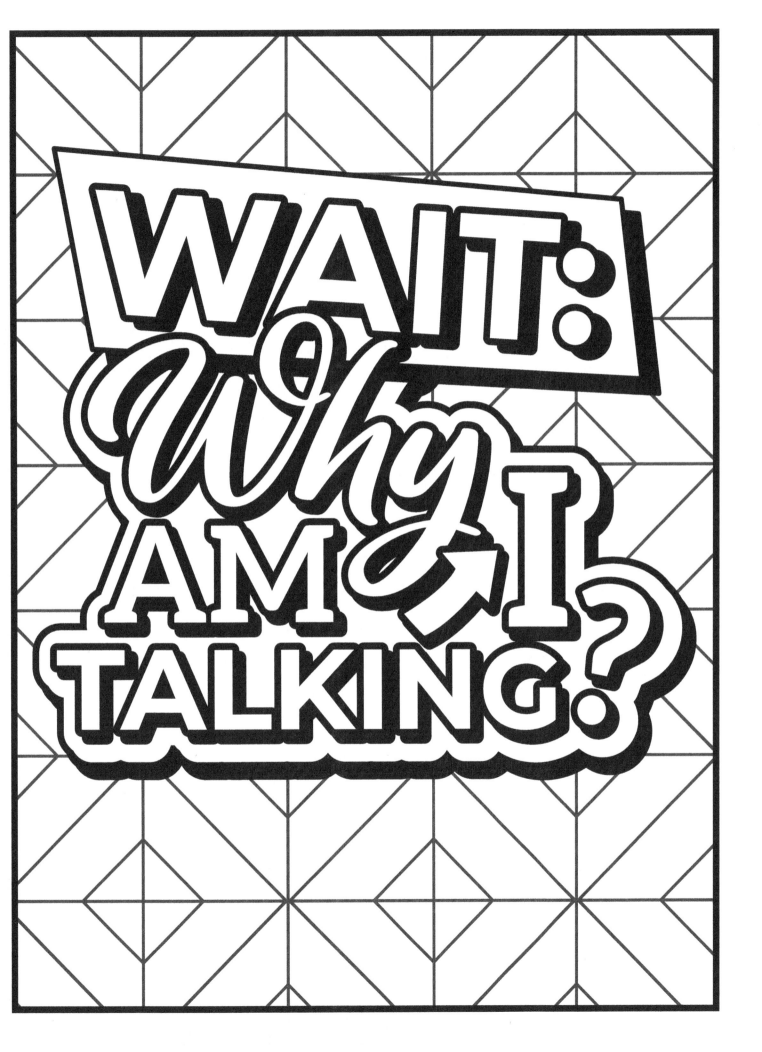

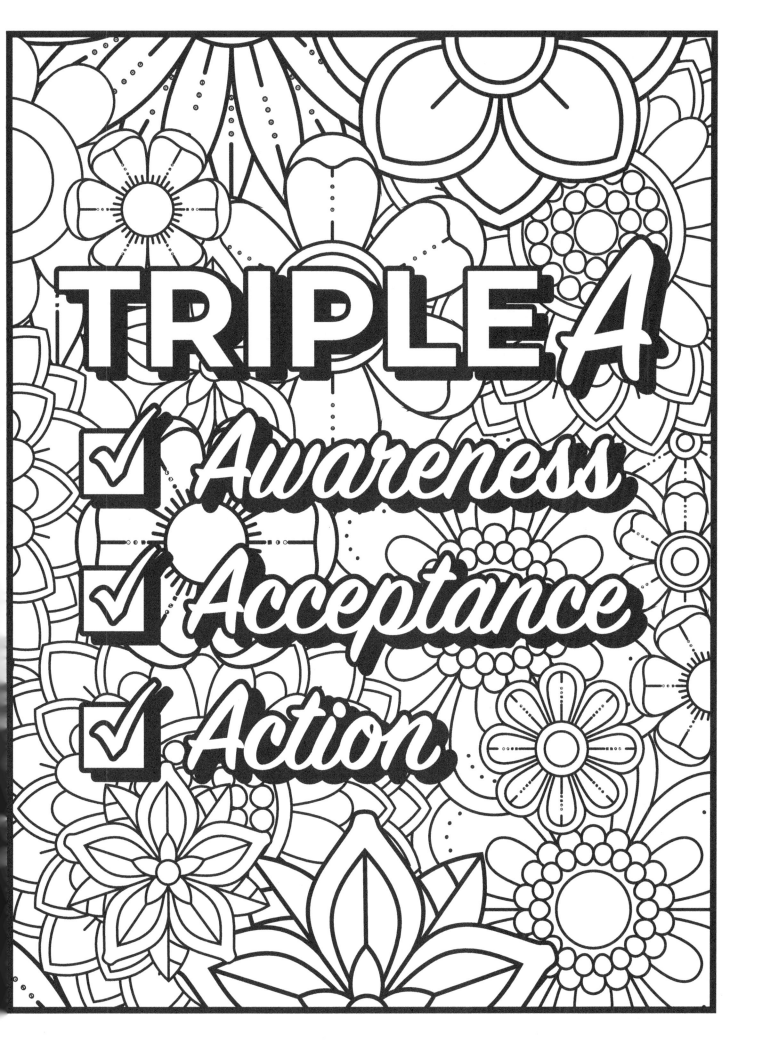

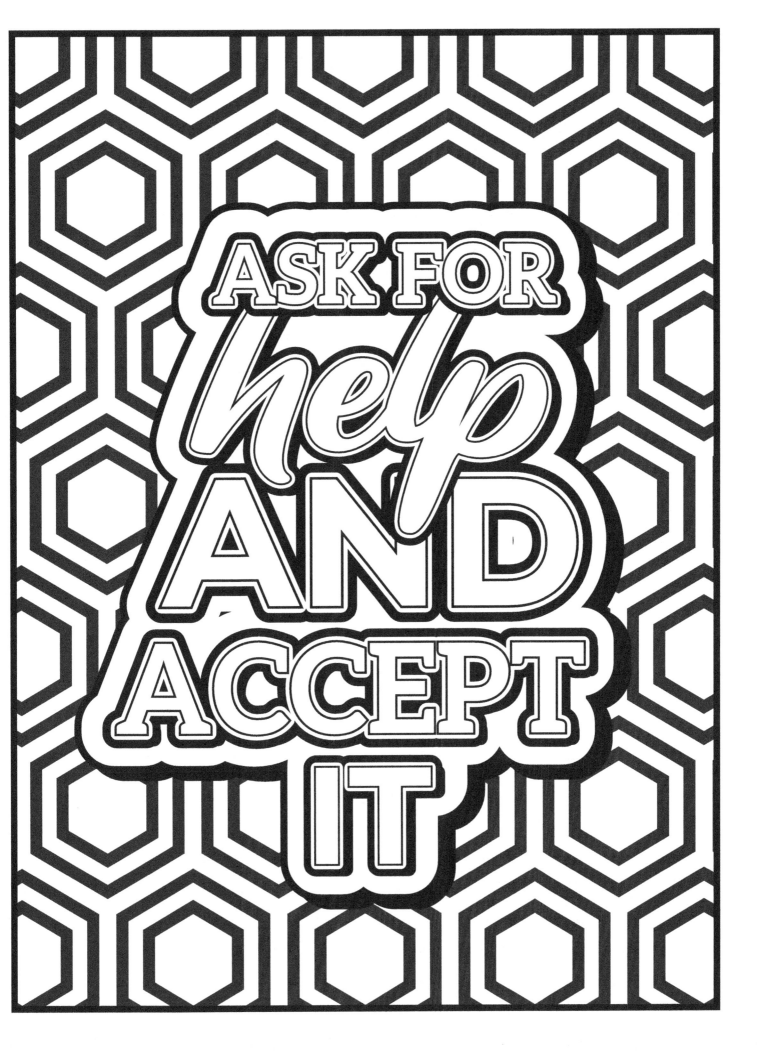

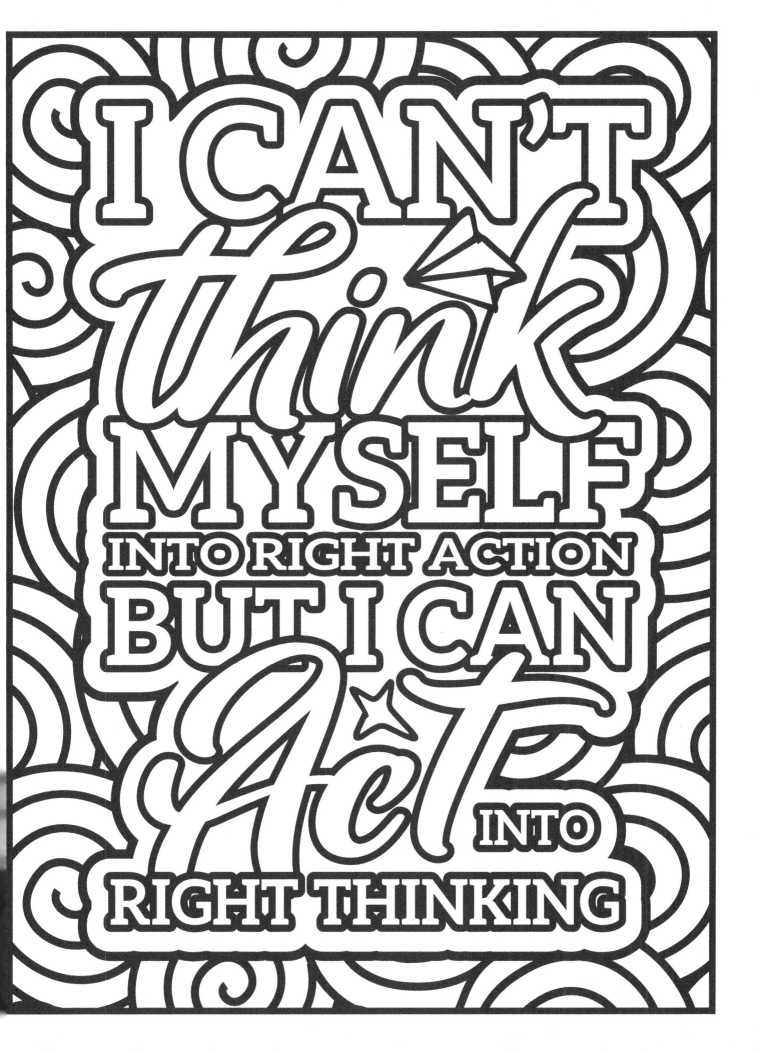

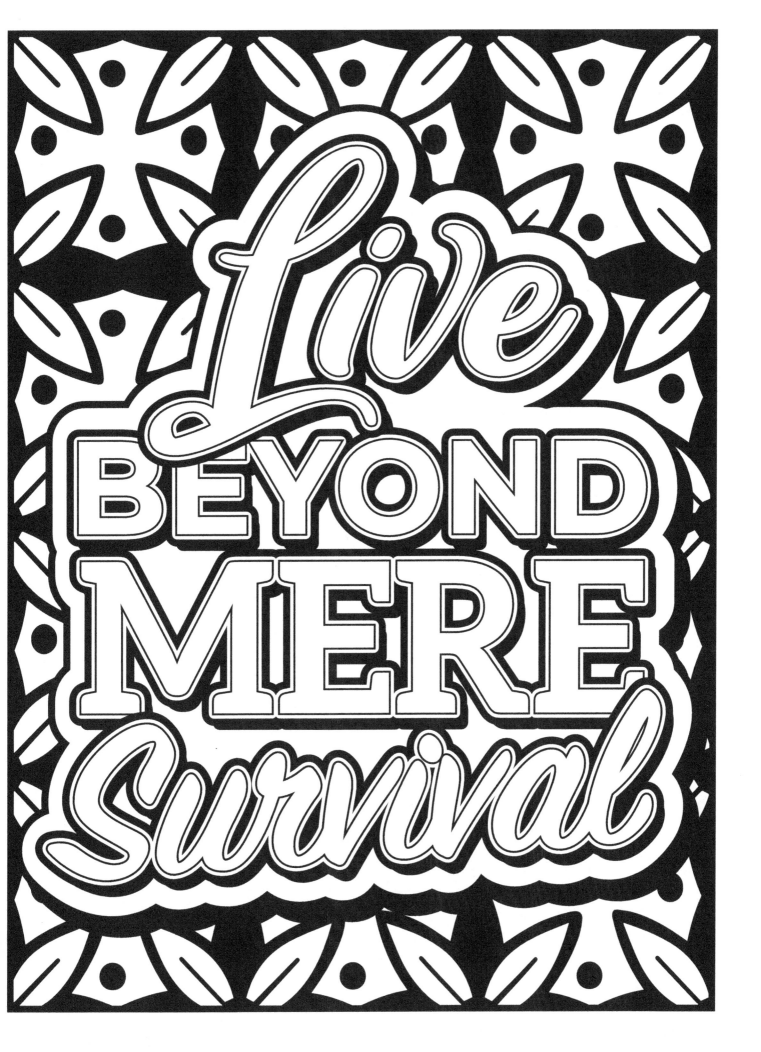

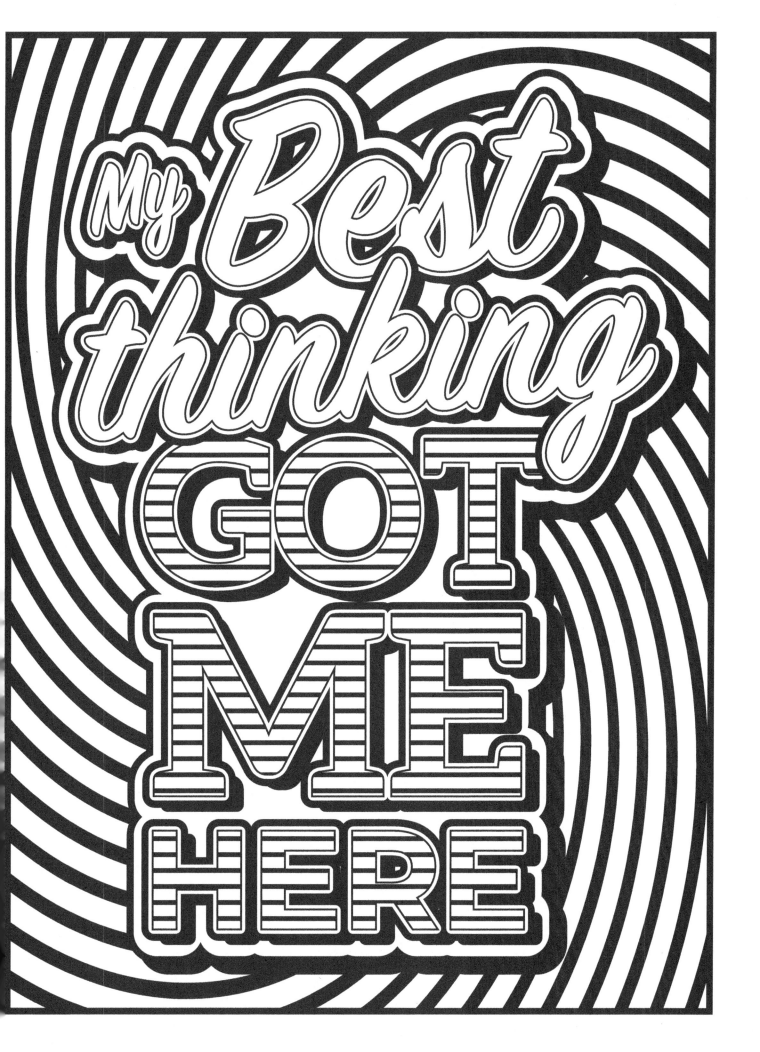

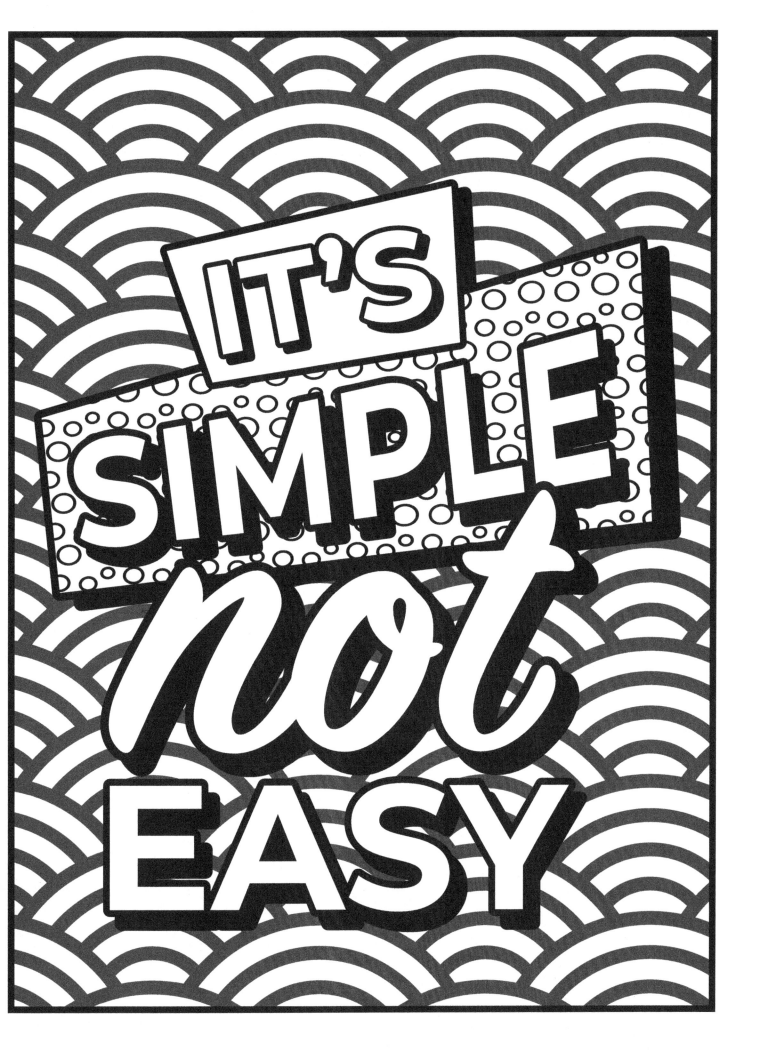

COLOR TEST PAGE

Made in the USA
Coppell, TX
07 November 2024

39825090R00063